Fun wit
HIDDEN PICTURE PUZZLES
Coloring Book

Jill Droppa

DOVER PUBLICATIONS, INC.
New York

NOTE

Here are 24 hidden picture puzzles to test your powers of perception. The scenes feature some favorite animals—zebras, deer, giraffes, lions and more. Some are shown in their natural habitat, while others are doing some pretty unusual things: monkeys playing baseball, sea horses wearing cowboy clothes and alligators playing at the beach. All of the scenes are filled with hidden surprises: numbers, letters, animals, articles of clothing and household objects. Captions beneath each scene will tell you what to look for. After you've found the hidden items, you can color the drawings in. (If you get stuck, solutions for the puzzles are provided in the back of the book.)

Published in Canada by General Publishing Company, Ltd., 30 Lesmill Road, Don Mills, Toronto, Ontario.
Published in the United Kingdom by Constable and Company, Ltd., 3 The Lanchesters, 162–164 Fulham Palace Road, London W6 9ER.

Bibliographical Note

Fun with Hidden Picture Puzzles Coloring Book is a new work, first published by Dover Publications, Inc., in 1996.

International Standard Book Number: 0-486-28826-9

Manufactured in the United States of America
Dover Publications, Inc., 31 East 2nd Street, Mineola, N.Y. 11501

The elephants have arrived at their favorite watering hole. Help them find the following hidden items: **a squirrel, a snowman, a pair of scissors, a dog, a worm, a bird, a carrot, two rabbits, an apple and a needle.**

Join these dogs for the hunt! See if you can find **a bell, a heart, a carrot, two mushrooms, an elf's slipper, a beet, a watch, a hat, a rabbit, a chicken drumstick and a fish.**

There's more to this campfire scene than meets the eye. See if you can find **a flag, a mushroom, a baseball bat, a pear, a cup, a turtle, a pipe, a chicken drumstick, a rainbow and an elf's slipper.**

Here's a squirrely forest scene! Find **a rabbit, a beret, an alligator, a goose, a cup, a bird, a glove, a needle, a beet, a mitten and a feather.**

See if you can find the hidden objects in this scene: **a baseball bat, a snake, a shoe, a hat, a rabbit, a fork, a needle, a bone, an alligator and a goose.**

From their bird's-eye view, these high fliers can see a lot. Can you see **a fork, a needle, a pear, a rabbit, an envelope, a mouse, a pencil, a sailboat, a bear and a number 7?**

There are plenty of underwater surprises hidden in this watery Wild, Wild West. Find **a hockey stick, a penguin, a snail, a fish, a worm, a bell, a slice of pepperoni pizza, a ladle and a wrench.**

See if you can "spot" the hidden objects in this picture: **a flower, a toothbrush, a hat, a butterfly, a carrot, a mushroom, a mitten, a hand bell, a boot, a bow and a sock.**

This garden has grown some surprises. Find the hidden objects: **a glove, a lit candle, an ax, a slice of pepperoni pizza, a match stick, a squirrel, an envelope, a mushroom, a needle and a book.**

This goose and her goslings are amazed that there are so many hidden objects nearby. Can you find **a heart, a boot, an acorn, a thumbtack, a carrot, a pair of scissors, a needle, a hat, an ax and a spoon?**

These zany zebras have lots to laugh about. Join the fun and find **a duck, two fish, a teddy bear, a needle, a mitten, a number 2, a bird, a letter Y and a candy cane.**

Help these sleepy lions find the hidden objects so they can get some rest: **a sailboat, a feather, a hat, a mushroom, a bone, a heart, a dog, a sock, a beet, a rabbit and an inchworm.**

While these hatchlings are busy eating their dinner, see how many of these hidden objects you can find: **a cup, a squirrel, a flag, a ring, a fish, a pencil, an ear of corn, a needle, a sailboat, a pear, a pin and a glove.**

These wolf cubs are too busy playing to look for the hidden objects. See if you can find them: **a comb, a snowman, a mushroom, a heart, a bird, a beet, a swan, a needle, a fish and a carrot.**

Playing 'possom is almost as fun as looking for the hidden objects. Find **two fish, a hat, a fork, a cane, a rabbit, a wrench, a pipe, a beet, a needle, a penguin and a squirrel.**

There's more to having fun in the sun than these gators know! Find **a butterfly, a carrot, an elephant, a lady's hat, a needle, a fish, a cup, a heart, a mushroom, a shark and a ring.**

Basking in the desert heat, these lizards are unaware of the hidden objects around them. See if you can find **a pipe, a mushroom, a ring, an umbrella, a cap, a light bulb, a number 2, a number 7, a lady's shoe, a cup, a fish and an ax.**

Look carefully at this forest scene to find the hidden objects: **a slice of bread, two butterflies, a rabbit, a lamb, a cap, a letter Y, a mouse, a squirrel and a fish.**

Help this happy couple celebrate their wedding by finding **a ladle, two birds, a turtle, a butterfly, a ring, a baseball bat, a light bulb, a wrench and a shoe.**

Here's a funny bit of monkey business. Find the following hidden objects while the monkeys play ball: **a slice of pepperoni pizza, a ladle, a lady's hat, a cup, a rabbit, an envelope, an inchworm, a mouse, a snake and an ax.**

These turtles are having a great time at the playground. While they play, see if you can find **a mitten, a chick, a match stick, a glove, a mushroom, a bird, a lady's shoe, an ice cream cone, an elephant, a slice of bread, a cup and a rabbit.**

While these butterflies are busy sipping nectar, find the hidden objects: **a bow, a mitten, a brush, a mouse, a performing seal, a number 2, a heart, a needle, a cup, a rabbit, a bell and a bird.**

This mouse has found a snack, and the toad has found a comfortable seat; see if you can find **a slice of pepperoni pizza, a needle, a heart, a worm, a man's hat, a lady's hat, a bell, a bird, a lady's shoe and a sock.**

Join in the fun at the Polar Swim Club. Find **a bell, a pear, an acorn, a pipe, a caterpillar, a worm, a flower, a rabbit, a hat, a mitten and a bird.**

SOLUTIONS

page 1

page 2

page 3

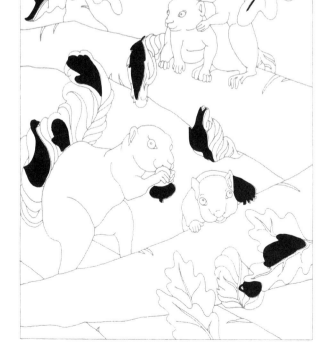

page 4

page 5

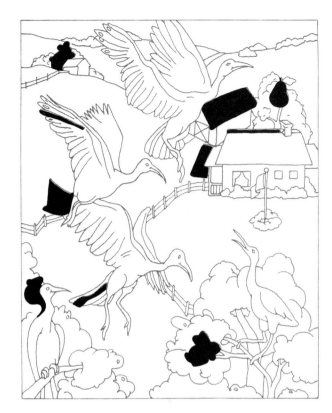

page 6

page 7

page 8

26

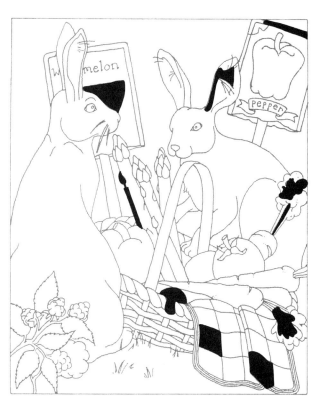

page 9

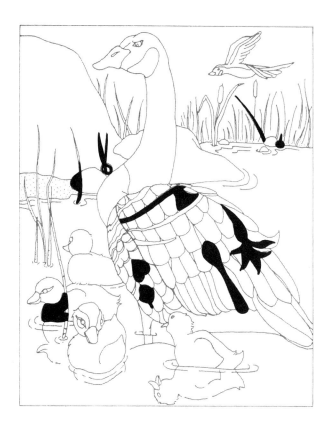

page 10

page 11

page 12

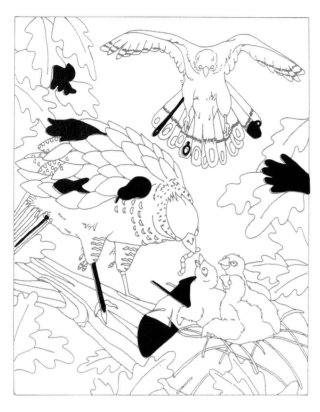

page 13

page 14

page 15

page 16

page 17

page 18

page 19

page 20

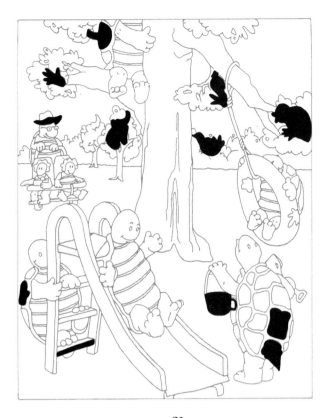

page 21

page 22

page 23

page 24